TH
AND
THE COLLIERY

THE CROSS
AND
THE COLLIERY

Tom Wright

Bishop of Durham

First published in Great Britain in 2007

Society for Promoting Christian Knowledge
36 Causton Street
London SW1P 4ST

British Library Cataloguing-in-Publication Data
A catalogue record for this book is available from the British Library

ISBN 978–0–281–05971–3

1 3 5 7 9 10 8 6 4 2

Typeset by Graphicraft Ltd, Hong Kong
Printed in Great Britain by CPI Bookmarque, Croydon, CR0 4TD

Produced on paper from sustainable forests

For the people of Easington Colliery
and in particular the Church of the Ascension

Contents

Contents

Photographs

Easington Colliery shaft headgear

Introduction

In Holy Week 2007 I invited myself to the Church of the Ascension, Easington Colliery, to share in the life of the church (part of the United Benefice of Easington, Easington Colliery and South Hetton) as they journeyed from Palm Sunday through to Good Friday and then on to Easter Day. I am especially grateful to the Rector of Easington, the Revd Brian E. Close, to his wife Angie, to the churchwardens of the Church of the Ascension, Mildred Bridges and John Pearce, to the various parishioners who looked after me and supplied endless tea and coffee, to the staff of Rutherford House where we stopped in for a meal, to the children who welcomed me to their Fun Day, to the local government officials (especially Tony Foster), leaders, politicians and activists who sat me down and told me what they were trying to do in one of the toughest wards in the country, to the staff at the Miners' Welfare for their friendly hospitality, and to the whole community for welcoming their bishop into their midst.

Easington Colliery – that's the name of the town, sometimes abbreviated simply to 'the Colliery', not just of the old pit – sits near the bottom of the hill as you come down from Easington Village, looking out across the North Sea. On a clear day, looking south, you can see not only to Hartlepool and the mouth of the River Tees but also to the North Yorkshire cliffs beyond. It is a classic County Durham scene: great beauty all around, gritty industry – or its legacy – in the foreground.

The image that most people now have of Easington Colliery is from the film *Billy Elliot*, significant parts of which were shot in the old streets of the Colliery, some (but not all) of which have now been demolished. The locals are partly proud of that link with sudden fame, but also angry at one impression the film wrongly gave. In the scenes in Billy's home, his father and other adults would frequently use strong, unpleasant and violent language. That, I was told again and again, was simply untrue to how things were. There was a very definite and proud code of behaviour. Easington Colliery was the sort of place where everybody knew everybody else, where you could leave your front door unlocked day and night, and where – though miners would no doubt use interesting language down the pit from time to time – there was a clear rule about what you would and wouldn't say in front of women or children.

That little wrinkle tells its own story, especially when you contrast it with how things are today; and that brings us to the most important fact about Easington Colliery and why I chose to speak there in the way I did in Holy Week 2007. Easington pit was one of the last to close. Its range was enormous, with seams going out for miles under the North Sea. Despite splendid efforts in the wake of the devastating 1984 miners' strike, efforts which saw the pit's output increase by leaps and bounds and more than keep pace with the 'targets' that were imposed from outside, the Government announced in 1992 that it was going to shut the pit, and on 30 April 1993 the last coal was drawn. The pit was then razed to the ground in 1994, and the entire area was grassed over. It feels like a graveyard. The whole area, where once there was a busy and highly productive pit employing thousands, sits there quietly at the east end of Easington Colliery, beside the railway line and looking out to sea. It carries an eerie sense of bereavement, of the heart having been ripped out of the community.

This extraordinary and bewildering sense of loss is highlighted by the social effects of removing not only the main employer but also the main source of income from the whole community. The bustling, lively main street now has several shops boarded up. The old school, substantial and solidly built, is now a large, ugly shell, a target for vandals and a daily reminder to the whole town of what once was and is now no more. The Council has done great things with a new school and other amenities, but the signs of a great disaster are all around. In the old streets, some houses are derelict, others used as bases for drug dealers who do an all-too-brisk trade in the area, others still inhabited by long-time residents who don't want to leave their homes of many decades but are in some cases afraid to walk down their own streets. In most of the calculations of 'social deprivation' – drug and alcohol abuse, teenage pregnancy, obesity and sheer poverty itself – the council ward of Easington comes at or near the bottom of the pile, and Easington Colliery is one of the most deprived parts of that ward. There are some splendid community initiatives – I was there to witness the opening of a new sports facility – but you have a sense that these valiant efforts are simply raising small flags of hope beside the much larger and more powerful symbols of deprivation and despair.

The theme of bereavement has a particular resonance for Easington Colliery. On 29 May 1951, at 4.45 a.m., just as the night shift was leaving and the early morning shift arriving, there was a large underground explosion. Families and friends gathered in large numbers at the pit gates, and gradually the news emerged that 81 miners and 2 rescue workers had died. The last body was not brought out for over a fortnight. A Memorial Avenue of 83 trees was planted, leading south-east from near the church and ending up looking out over the sea. In due course two or three of the trees needed replacing; I had the privilege of replanting them, with the help of a group of schoolchildren and a large crowd of onlookers, including many families who could remember men lost in the disaster, and one of the men who had been part of the rescue team all those years before.

Easington Colliery, being a development from Easington Village, didn't have its own church until 1913. (St Mary's Church in Easington Village itself has a list of Rectors going back to the twelfth century, including some who went on to be bishops, cardinals or even archbishops, and others who became famous without achieving high office, such as Bernard Gilpin in the sixteenth century and H. G. Liddell in the nineteenth – the Liddell, that is, whose daughter Alice was celebrated, after the family's move to Oxford, in Lewis Carroll's *Alice in Wonderland*.) The pit had opened in the late nineteenth century, and by the early years of the twentieth it was obvious that a new church was badly needed in the area. The Church of the Ascension was built in 1929 to replace the original Mission Church of 1913, and was opened on Ascension Day 1929 by the then Bishop of Durham, Hensley Henson. It stands in a prominent position overlooking the main street, and boasts some wonderful features including a fine screen. Parts of the interior were richly redecorated, in memory of those who died in the 1951 disaster, by Sir Ninian Comper. The church has a rich tradition of standing at the heart of the old mining community, which is symbolized by its own unique cross made out of miners' pickaxes.

But this raises the uncomfortable and tricky question: what is a town like this all about, once the mines have gone? How can the church play an appropriate part in helping a town at a time like this? Can the community spirit, so rich and important through the years of dangerous but productive work, be recaptured once it has escaped? What is there for young people now to do – especially since the laissez-faire official policy about housing, following the selling off of the old council houses, means that it is harder and harder for couples starting out to afford their own home in their own town?

There is no easy answer to these questions, and I pay tribute to generations of council officials, union members and officials, politicians and others who, mostly local people themselves, have known perfectly well what the problems were and struggled hard to find solutions. But I believe – and this was the real impetus for these talks – that part of the problem may be in the difficulty of moving forwards when all the symbols and local culture are pointing back. As with an individual who has lost someone they love, part of the point of the process of grief, painful and horrible though it is, is to enable the person eventually to look about them, draw a deep breath, and make some new starts.

This isn't just a matter of 'moving on', in the fashionable jargon. It's a matter of looking the past in the face, owning up to the grief which we often hide, and so laying a more solid foundation for what may be to come. I decided therefore that it was worth spending some time in facing the multiple bereavements of Easington Colliery and in weaving them together with the story of all stories, the story of Jesus on his way to the cross. As I say more than once in what follows, I have no blueprint for what might or should happen next. If God is at work he will do what he will do, and his purposes are always full of surprises. But I am convinced that when we bring our griefs and sorrows within the story of God's own grief and sorrow, and allow them to be held there, God is able to bring healing to us and new possibilities to our lives. That is, of course, what Good Friday and Easter are all about.

I hope that what was said then, in one very particular and specific situation, may perhaps carry helpful resonances for people in other times and places who, though facing different kinds of sorrow and puzzlement, may need to tread a similar pathway. The talks were based on the passages of scripture referred to at the start of each section, and it would be a good idea to read them through, slowly and thoughtfully, before reading the section itself. (The poem at the end of Chapter 7, 'A meditation on Holy Saturday', by the way, is my own, taken from *Easter Oratorio*, for which Paul Spicer wrote the music.) And I invite the reader of this book, whether or not they live in a community similar to Easington Colliery, to 'listen in' as the people of that community and I made our way through the week, writing down particular sorrows and laying them at the foot of the cross, and to reflect on how that particular journey is reflected in many other situations of personal and corporate grief, and how it can lead, eventually, to the rebirth of signs of hope. (All proceeds from this book, by the way, will go towards further efforts to make those 'signs of hope' happen within the parish of Easington, and particularly in Easington Colliery itself.)

The talks that follow were only one part of what was going on that week. I hope they will serve as a reminder to those who heard them, and as a pointer to those who didn't, that what we were all trying to do was to listen to the pain and grief of a community in the trauma that goes with the break-up of an old way of life, and the puzzle about what, if anything, can replace it – and to bring that pain into the presence of God through the journey of Jesus to the cross. That process is all about listening, prayer, reflection, walking about, discussing and looking for signs of hope. These talks were the tip of the iceberg, but it's the iceberg itself that really matters. Mind you, 'iceberg' is a pretty bad illustration for Easington Colliery. Despite all the sad and painful things that have happened there over recent years, you still get one of the warmest welcomes in the country.

Tom Wright
Auckland Castle

1

A SERMON AT
THE EUCHARIST
ON PALM SUNDAY

Easington Colliery, early 1900s

Making the journey, singing the song (Isaiah 50.4–9a; Philippians 2.5–11; Luke 23.1–49)

There's a little game which church folk sometimes play with each other. Someone reads a line from the middle of a hymn and then you have to work out what the first line of the hymn is. It's often quite hard, even when you know the hymn quite well.

So if I said,

> What may I say?
> Heaven was his home,
> But mine the tomb
> Wherein he lay.

... someone would probably be able to say, 'My song is love unknown'. And if I said, 'The last and fiercest strife is nigh', I suspect someone would be able to say, 'Ride on! ride on in majesty'. And of course many churches, in many traditions, regularly sing both of those on Palm Sunday, setting the tone for worship throughout the coming 'Holy Week', the greatest week in the church's year.

There's a harder version of the same game. If I hum the tune of a well-known hymn, most regular worshippers will probably work out what it is (assuming I hum it sufficiently clearly and accurately!). But supposing I were to hum, not the tune itself, but one of the other parts – the alto, tenor or bass? That wouldn't be so easy, would it? But without those parts the tune wouldn't sound quite the same, and it probably wouldn't mean quite the same thing.

One of the mysteries of music is that we can't, as individuals, sing more than one note at the same time. The organist can play several notes all together, but left to ourselves we can only manage one; so we need each other to make up the harmony. Sometimes we sing in two-part harmony. Often hymns and other songs have four parts, the treble (which normally has the tune), the alto, the tenor and the bass. But you can have a lot more. Thomas Tallis, one of the greatest composers of the Elizabethan age, once wrote a motet with no fewer than *forty* parts, all different, all harmonizing together.

What we're going to do in these meditations is to learn to sing a song together. No, I don't mean a literal song. We may find ourselves singing one or two new things during Holy Week, but that's not what I'm saying. We're going on a journey: the journey which starts today, Palm Sunday, with Jesus riding into Jerusalem on the donkey and the crowds singing 'Hosanna'; and we're going to be following the story of Jesus as he goes on his way to the cross, today in Luke and then for the next five days in John. And we're going to see this astonishing and moving story as a great tune, a theme which rises and falls and grows and swells and comes to its climax of course on Good Friday itself. And we shall be here listening to that tune and finding our hearts once again stirred by it.

But if the story of Jesus from Palm Sunday to Good Friday is the tune, what is the harmony, and how can we learn to sing it together? This is where we have to remind ourselves of one of the main points the early Christians never tired of repeating and exploring. If the main tune is the story of Jesus, the bass part – the musical line which grounds the whole thing and keeps it solid and firm – is the Old Testament. When the first Christians produced a summary of the gospel, it began like this: Christ died for our sins *according to the scriptures*. And this doesn't mean 'according to' in the sense that we sometimes say 'according to the *Sun*, the lads played well, but according to the

Mirror, they were rubbish' – in other words, 'Well, the scriptures say so, but they might be wrong.' No: what they meant was that Jesus was the Christ, Israel's Messiah, and his death was *in accordance with* the scriptures. In other words, if you want to know what his death meant, you have to hear the music, to listen not just to the tune which says 'Christ died', but to the harmony which says 'and this is what it means'.

And that is why we shall listen in particular to parts of the book of Isaiah: four short poems, in fact, which stand near the heart of the Old Testament and draw together a great deal of what it's saying. We'll be looking at them a bit more closely in Chapters 2, 3, 4 and 7. And the main reason we go back to these poems is that all the signs are that Jesus himself had those poems in mind as he went up to Jerusalem for that last journey. He had plenty of other scriptures in his head and heart as well, of course, not least the Psalms, Psalms like the one which spoke of pilgrims going up to Jerusalem singing, 'Blessed is the one who comes in the name of the Lord'. And when we take all these and other scriptures, and learn to listen to them while we're listening to the main tune, the story of Jesus, we discover that this story wasn't just the tale of a young man cruelly victimized, unjustly tried and executed, suffering at the hands of callous and brutal authorities and soldiers. It is all that, of course, as well; but underneath, down in the bass part where the harmony is held secure, it is the story of the love of God the creator for his suffering world. That's the story the Old Testament tells, the deep, dark tune that forms the bass part for the tune which Jesus himself will then sing.

No other holy book, no other philosophical text, no other collection of wise sayings, sings a tune quite like this. If you try to listen to Jesus' song with any of those other tunes as the bass part, it'll mean something different. It's in the Old Testament that we find the story which speaks about a God who made the world, and who loved the world so much that when his human creatures rebelled he called a special people to help him set the world right again; and when this special people, too, rebelled, he didn't abandon the plan, but stuck with it, and with them, and promised that he would be with them, with them in person, to see the thing through, to take the weight of that rebellion and its consequences on to himself so that he could set his people right, and so that he could set the world right. That is the great story the Old Testament tells, and it tells it most clearly through the poems in Isaiah which will form the bass part for our reflection. And if we're going to understand the tune we sing – the story of Jesus himself – we need to listen to that bass part as well.

But of course this isn't just two-part harmony. There are plenty of other parts to this song, and I'm just going to mention two of them now, because they are hugely important as well for us as we make this journey together. The next part – think of it as the tenor, if you like, the one that often tells you if the chord is major or minor, happy or sad – the next part is the story of our own world and our own community. Part of the challenge of Holy Week is that when we hear the tune of Jesus going up to Jerusalem and on to his death, and when we listen to the Old Testament which helps us make sense of it, we don't use this as a way of escaping from the realities of our world, but rather as the framework within which we can look at our world in a new way.

And our world – your world – today's global village, today's Western world, the north-east of England, the ward of Easington – has become a confused and dangerous and worrying place. The church in Easington Colliery stands in the middle of a community that has borne the brunt of the shifts that have taken place in our society, quite dramatic shifts of power and ways of life and traditional values. Philosophers sit in comfortable chairs in Oxford, Paris and Harvard and point out that people today don't know who they are any more. People in communities like Easington experience that as a daily reality.

That's why there is poverty and crime and obesity and drugs and the breakdown of social fabric.

And part of the challenge for us during Holy Week is to hear that story – the story of the pain of the world, of *our* world – going on *within* the music of Jesus' story and the Old Testament story, like the tenor part between the treble and the bass. There are various ways of doing this in a very practical manner, and this is what I suggest for this week, in this church. I want you to gather up the pain and grief of this community: the mining disaster half a century ago when over 80 men lost their lives; the other mining disaster – the pit closures – of 20 or 30 years ago, when nearly twenty times that number lost their jobs and the community lost its heart; the unemployment and poverty, the family and social sorrows, whatever they may be. I want you to write down, some time over the next two or three days, just a sentence or two, or maybe just a word or two, about the particular griefs that this community has had to bear in recent years. And over the course of the week we'll gather them up, we'll put them in a basket here somewhere, and when we get to Good Friday we'll bring them to the cross and we'll leave them there.

Because, you see, that is the only way we can really and truly deal with them. We come, like the crowds on Palm Sunday, with all kinds of hopes and frustrations, with sorrows and fears, and we have that glimmer of hope that maybe Jesus will be able to do something about it all. But the only way it'll happen is by singing that story within the music that's framed by Jesus' story during this week, and by the Old Testament which provides the bass line of the harmony. So I want you to scribble something down – it doesn't have to be fancy, we won't read them out – and bring it tomorrow or one of the days, and we'll keep them here and fold them into the story on Good Friday itself. I have no idea what God will do with them. But I do know that, when you bring things to the foot of the cross, the music of Jesus' death transforms them in ways we can't predict or explain.

But there's one more part in this song, and it's very personal. Call it the alto part if you like – sometimes a bit shy, sometimes doesn't seem very exciting, but the harmony isn't complete without it, and sometimes it has spectacular things to do. This is your part, your own personal story, your private bit of the song. As we listen to the main tune, Jesus on his journey to Jerusalem and Calvary; as we listen to the bass part, the Old Testament which grounds the whole thing; as we reflect on the tenor part, the story of our whole community; so we have to bring our own story and learn to sing it within this total music. The world all around us is giving us other music and telling us we have to keep in harmony with that. We are making this journey with Jesus this week because we want to learn again how to keep in with his song, with his story.

That's often difficult. Frequently it's a painful thing to do. We may be happy one minute, like the Palm Sunday crowds, and angry the next, like the Good Friday crowds. We may be sad or puzzled or confused or fearful or whatever. But this is the week, above all, when we sing our own private song and we try and get it in harmony again with Jesus' song, with God's song. That is the journey that we are making together this week, me as well as you. And we'll sing it today and then again on Good Friday:

> My song is love unknown,
> My saviour's love to me . . .
> Here might I stay and sing
> No story so divine;
> Never was love, dear King,
> Never was grief like thine.

And as we learn to sing his song, to listen for the full harmony, and to supply the part in the middle which only we can know and sing, we find ourselves surrounded, enfolded, welcomed, challenged, healed and transformed by a love we can find nowhere else: the love of Jesus himself, embodying the love of the one true God.

2

A MEDITATION ON THE MONDAY OF HOLY WEEK

Easington Colliery, 1920s

The Servant who announces new things (Isaiah 42.1–9; John 12.1–11)

In the previous chapter, I wrote of the way in which the story of Jesus works upon us like a tune. We hear the story, we feel it unfold like a rich, warm, strange but beautiful melody, and we pause and ask ourselves what it means. And part of the answer to that question comes in the bass part of the composition, which is what we find in the Old Testament. Matthew, Mark, Luke and John didn't want their readers just to listen to the tune they were playing; they wanted us to hear it as the new top line for an older and darker music.

Put it the other way round, if you like. Supposing you came across one of those karaoke records where they've recorded all the backing but not the song itself, because you're supposed to sing that. But supposing you'd never heard the song and didn't know either the words or the tune. You'd be stuck – but also frustrated, because the backing music might sound really good. Then at last someone comes and sings the song to you; and you don't just think, 'Hey! That's a great song!' You think, 'Of course! That's what it was all about!' The backing and the song are quite different. But they're made for each other.

Out of all the Old Testament, Jesus made the central part of the book of Isaiah especially his own, not least the four poems which people today sometimes call the 'Servant Songs'. Putting this together with a bit of John's gospel invites us to see Isaiah 42 as the backing music, and John 12 as the tune.

15

And quite a tune it is. One of the most intimate and gentle, and yet sharply striking, snapshots of Jesus anywhere in his ministry. Jesus is at dinner with Mary, Martha and Lazarus – Lazarus, whom he has only just raised from the dead. Mary blows a year's worth of wages by pouring wonderful ointment over Jesus' feet and wiping them with her hair. In the next chapter Jesus is going to wash the disciples' feet, but here he has his washed in advance by Mary. It's a moving and emotional moment, with both of them deeply vulnerable; and we feel we'd like to stay and think about it a bit longer, and allow the tune to wind itself deeper into our imagination . . .

But we can't, because like someone picking up the radio and angrily throwing it out of the window, Judas cuts across the music and tells them both off. 'What are you playing at? Don't you care about the poor? This is sheer waste!' How to spoil a party in one easy lesson. But Jesus doesn't shout back. Instead, he points to a deeper reality which certainly Judas, and presumably Mary, hadn't seen coming. 'She was getting my body ready for burial. It was a kind of advance anointing. Yes, the poor really do matter. But this needed to be done.' And now we are back at the music again, only this time at a different point in the tune. The intimacy, the vulnerability of Jesus – and of Mary! – suddenly become pointers forward to Jesus no longer barefoot at the dinner party but naked on the cross.

And as we listen to this tune and try to remember it, we hear the accompaniment which Isaiah provides. 'Look!' he says, in the name of God, 'Here is my servant.' And we look, and we see a strange and important sight. One of the most important truths in the whole Bible is that the God who made the world has promised to set it right at last, one day: to sort out the mess, to put everything to rights, to fill the world with his justice and mercy. And if we know our business we long for that day and pray for it, because the world is full of violence and injustice and idolatry and immorality. God's good creation is defaced.

Human beings who bear God's image are treated shamefully. And God has promised to set all that right at last.

And the point about Isaiah's poem is that *God will send his servant to get this project under way.* 'Here is my servant; I will put my Spirit upon him, and he will bring justice to the nations . . . he will not falter, or be discouraged, till he establishes justice on the earth; and in his law the islands will put their hope.' In other words: in advance of the final day, when God sorts everything out, the Servant is going to undertake to get going with the business, to put it in hand and give it its decisive start. And because this work will involve bringing peace to the world, the Servant will do his work in a peaceful and gentle manner. He won't raise his voice or yell. He won't go shouting around the streets. And he won't be brutal or arrogant with those who are feeling their way towards the light. He is doing, explains Isaiah, a new thing; and he's doing it in a new way. Those of us who long to see God at work doing new things in our communities, and in our lives, would do well to listen.

Do you begin to see how this song stands behind John 12 and makes sense of it? And as we put Isaiah and John together, side by side, we glimpse one answer at least to the old question: But who is the Servant?

From Isaiah's point of view, the Servant is a bit like a king, an ideal king of Israel who will do justice and mercy at last. But the Servant is more than just an individual. He seems to take on the role God mapped out for Israel as a whole. From the prophet's point of view, the Servant Songs are like a job description in an advertisement: 'Wanted! A Servant for the Lord!' But the prophet wrote a job description for which there could, eventually, be only one appropriate applicant. And here he is: Jesus, not raising his voice, not joining Judas in telling Mary off, but with his eyes fixed on his strange work of setting the world right, and doing so, as we see, through his own death.

We'll come to why that had to be in the following chapters. But for now, let's see how we're getting on with the other two parts of the music. If the story of Jesus is the tune, and the poem of Isaiah is the bass part, where are we in the middle?

Our world today, perhaps especially in parts of our community where there has been a lot of sadness and loss, is full of signs that things need to be set right. When you walk down the street and see shops with steel shutters; when you drive past big buildings all boarded up; when you see groups of young people with nothing to do but make trouble for themselves and others; when you find other young people moving away because they can't get work and they can't find anywhere to live; then you're looking at a world that needs putting right.

And because there's always money near the heart of the questions, people will grumble like Judas at what the church does: why are you bothering singing hymns and all that nonsense, making a fuss about Jesus when there are people in need out there? But the response of the church, to cut a long story short, is that if Jesus is the true Servant of the Lord, we, his people, are called here, in this community and every community, to carry on his work of setting things right – not in big, loud campaigns, or pretending that we know the answers to complicated questions, but in the quiet, steady work of coming alongside people in need or sorrow or pain, of praying for and with people in trouble or difficulty, of quietly bringing light into dark places and hope into sad lives. There is more to being the church than that, but not less. As the song puts it, 'This is our God, the Servant King; he calls us now to follow him.'

And what about the other tune, the private and personal one? Well, I guess one way of getting at that, as we move forward in Holy Week, is to ask: who do you identify with in the story of Jesus, Mary, Martha, Lazarus and Judas?

Many of us, I suspect, identify with Martha. Here are we, getting on with the work; and here's someone else, my sister, making a fuss, putting on a display, attention-seeking as usual. Well, try living within the story – pause and watch as Jesus says what he says – and see what he might have to say to you. Or maybe you are more like Mary herself, ready to go and show how much you love Jesus. Fine, but don't be surprised if some people grumble. Maybe some of us are like Judas, always so worried about counting pennies – and perhaps so embarrassed by other people's emotions – that we'll get cross when anyone takes Jesus deeply seriously and personally. Maybe there's a bit of these, and more, in most of us.

But, for now, let's be clear that we *do* belong in this picture. And let's be clear, too, that Jesus is calling us to go forward with him into the rest of the week. He is calling us to see him as the Servant who has put things right by his death; and to see him, therefore, as the one who can set us right individually, and through the work he gives us to do can help to set things right in the world, in the wider community, in the lives of others who need him so much. This is our God, the Servant King; he calls us now to follow him.

3

A MEDITATION ON THE
TUESDAY OF HOLY WEEK

Group at pit head after disaster, 1951

The grain of wheat
(Isaiah 49.1–7; John 12.20–36)

———•◆•———

'Unless a grain of wheat falls into the earth and dies,' said Jesus, 'it remains just a single grain; but if it dies, it bears much fruit' (John 12.24). And straight away my mind goes to the heart of the problems which we have faced here in the North East, problems of which your local heartache here has been a classic and sharply defined symptom. It's not 20 years since previous Bishops of Durham marched up and down the road here with all the local miners in an attempt to keep the pit open. And when all efforts failed, those of you who have lived through it all, and have seen and felt the pain and the sense of loss, have been – let's face it – through a major bereavement. And, as with all bereavements, those of us who didn't share it can only stand by and look on in respect and sorrow.

But in Holy Week of all times, what we can also do is to bring our sorrows, large and small, corporate and personal (because of course there are all kinds of personal sorrows woven into the larger texture of the community sorrow at this point, sorrow about loss of jobs and prosperity, sorrow about loss of loved ones who died younger than they might have through illnesses contracted down the pit, and so on) – what we can do is to bring all these sorrows on the journey with Jesus, the journey that takes him to Jerusalem and ultimately to Calvary outside the city wall. We can bring them here and leave them at the foot of the cross. Part of my prayer for this church, for this community, for all of you this week as together we worship and wonder, ponder and pray, and for all reading these words, is that our bringing of these pains before our loving Lord, and our folding of them into the story of his passion, may be part of the means by which new life may come.

It's over 50 years since the disaster of 1951. It's nearly 15 years since they closed the pit and grassed it over like a graveyard. And part of our vocation this Holy Week is to get our grief out in the open: to say to our God, as you do with any bereavement, 'Why did it have to happen like this? Why him, why them, why us, why now, why didn't you do something?' Those are the right questions, the natural questions, the questions we always ask when we face the sudden shock of bereavement. And if people have stopped asking those questions here in Easington, and in many other towns and villages up and down the country, it may be because they've dealt with the bereavement in a healthy way, or it may be because they've grassed over the memories as well but without dealing with them, without laying the sorrow before God and seeing it enfolded in the story of Jesus. It may be because, in our country as a whole, we have come dangerously close to forgetting that Jesus is the one who wept at the grave of his friend, the one who shares our griefs and carries our sorrows.

The reading from John offers a standing invitation to bring our stories and sorrows and see them folded into the story and sorrow of Jesus. 'Unless a grain of wheat falls into the earth and dies, it remains just a single grain; but if it dies, it bears much fruit.' Now that's all very well when you're planting a seed and you know what sort of a plant it's going to grow into. But Jesus was talking about something much more scary. He was talking about going to his own death.

As you see in the reading, this was Jesus' strange reply to the request that some Greeks could come and see him. Non-Jews wanting to see him? That's a sign of something new! But Jesus doesn't respond as we expect. He doesn't say, 'OK, let them come, that's fine.' He says, in effect, 'Yes; what I've come to do will indeed reach to the ends of the earth, in God's great project of justice and mercy. But it's not going to happen in a nice, smooth, easy fashion. The world as a whole, and the human race as a whole, is enslaved to a dark power, the power of corruption and selfishness, the power of Evil with a capital E. And the way in which I shall bring God's saving justice, and his severe, healing mercy to the whole world is not just by teaching a few more people. It will be through my death. The grain of wheat must die, so that it can bear more fruit, new fruit, fruit you wouldn't believe if someone tried to tell you about it.'

As before, the tune we hear in John's story of Jesus is filled out, backed up, by what we read in Isaiah, which here means the second of the Servant Songs. The servant knows it's his job to work for God's purpose, but he finds himself saying, 'I've been wasting my time! What was it all for? I have laboured in vain; I've spent my strength for nothing and vanity.' But then he goes on: 'My cause is with the Lord, and my reward with my God.' The whole point of the Servant Songs is that the work of the Servant is the means by which God will accomplish the rescue not only of Israel but also of the whole human race and the whole creation. And, strangely, it seems to be part of God's purpose that there will come a time when it looks as though the whole thing has gone down the tube. 'I've been wasting my time! What was it all about?' That's how Easington has felt for some years now. That's how a lot of people feel with the large and small sorrows of their ordinary life.

So this great biblical story, of God's purposes to set the whole world right going ahead, actually includes the strange, dark theme which says that the Servant who is to carry out God's mission will look as though he's failed. All he can do is to trust God, to commit his cause to God, to wait in utter faith. For Jesus, that meant going to his death, in obedience to the Servant-vocation. As he read the scriptures and listened to the voice of the one he called Abba, Father, he knew that this vocation was meant for him and him alone. He had to go ahead of us into the dark, to do the opposite of what people expected him to do, to suffer apparent failure, degradation and shame. As Isaiah had said, he was one deeply despised, abhorred by the nations, the slave of rulers. But as he goes he declares: 'Now is the judgement of this world! Now the ruler of this world will be driven out! And when I'm lifted up from the earth, I will draw all people to myself!' (John 12.31). Somehow, he is saying, it will look as though the powers of the world are passing judgment on me. But what will happen is that God will be judging them.

So here are we, a community of prayer at the heart of a community that's been in pain now for several years, a community that has borne the pain and carried the sorrow which has afflicted so many in our country and the Western world as massive shifts in industrial and economic life have brought misery and puzzlement and despair. What are we to do? We are called, in Holy Week, *to claim in prayer that victory over the powers which Jesus won on the cross*: to hold the grief and pain of the community, and of our own hearts, within the love which went to Calvary for us; to pray that as the grains of wheat fall into the earth and die they will bear much fruit; and to work for that fruit, that new hope, that regeneration at every level, which God will give in his own time and his own way.

The frustrating thing, as always, is that I don't know and you don't know how God is going to do new things here, in our own lives or our own communities. That is why we need to cling on for dear life to the story of Jesus, and to learn as best we can to see the story of our community, and the story of our personal lives, like two musical lines held in between the story of Jesus and the deep notes of the Old Testament which explain it and give it depth. And that is why we shall stand at the foot of the cross on Good Friday, to bring our griefs and sorrows, our bereavement and our puzzlement, to the one who has gone down into the darkness on our behalf. And as we learn to do that for ourselves, for our neighbours, for our community, we learn the lesson which we as Christian folk need to learn again and again: that unless a grain of wheat falls into the earth and dies it remains a single grain, but that if it dies it will bear much fruit.

4

A MEDITATION ON THE WEDNESDAY OF HOLY WEEK

Shotton Rescue Team, 1951

Betrayal and trial
(Isaiah 50.4–9; John 13.21–30)

———•◦•———

When we say, as we do in creeds and confessions of faith, that Jesus Christ 'died for our sins', we are making a statement which works at several levels at once. I suspect mostly we think, when we say that, of our sins as a rather large and shapeless cloud, full of nasty thoughts and actions and words, somehow landing on Jesus as he dies on the cross. We're not sure quite how it all 'works', but we know that somehow he died so that we can be free from it all. And that's fine as far as it goes. As we shall see on Good Friday itself, there is more to be said than that, but it's a start.

But the story of Jesus which we follow in Holy Week makes it clear that something more specific is going on as well. If you drew up a catalogue of the deepest and darkest sins the human race can commit, you might find that a good many of them feature in the story of Jesus' final days, and that they tend to have something to do with getting Jesus put on the cross.

Think about it. Lying, including false witness in a lawcourt. Yes, that's there. Injustice, and oppression of the weak by the strong and of the poor by the rich. Yes, that's there. Racial prejudice: that's certainly there, with Pilate sneering at the Jews in general and Jesus in particular as 'king of the Jews'. Idolatry: well, that's behind quite a lot of it, as the Romans idolize their own military might and their much-touted justice system. Love of power: certainly, that's what kept Caiaphas and his friends going. And there's plenty of others as well. And now we come to one of the nastiest of all: betrayal.

I confess I don't often watch soap operas – principally because I don't get time to watch much TV at all. But from time to time, glancing through the 'what's on' section, I notice the plot summaries for the various long-running soaps. Not infrequently the word 'betrayal' crops up, usually of course in the setting of a relationship. I suspect some of you could give me some examples from *EastEnders* or *Coronation Street* or one of the others. Well, those of us who are used to hearing the story of Judas Iscariot may be a bit hardened to it, and we need to remind ourselves what was actually happening.

Judas was one of Jesus' closest friends and trusted companions. Trusted? Yes: he kept the purse. He was the treasurer. Now of course when you make anyone a treasurer of anything, from the local bridge club to Chancellor of the Exchequer, you give them a great temptation to misuse their trust, but Jesus presumably had trusted Judas, at least in the beginning. We of course look back on the story and we know from early on that Judas was the traitor, but nobody else knew that at the time. In the story we've just read, when Jesus says 'One of you is going to betray me', they don't all turn round and point the finger at Judas and say, 'Oh yes, we all know who that's going to be.' They are all worried: it isn't going to be me, is it? Only Jesus knows. Judas is one of them. He has been part of it all, has seen Jesus heal lepers, preach the gospel, raise the dead. He's done it himself, casting out demons in Jesus' name, watching God's power do new things. And now . . .

We don't know why Judas did it. We do know that being betrayed by a very, very close friend is extremely nasty. Trust is one of the most precious things in human life; breaking trust is one of the most horrible. And the point I'm making is this: when we speak of Jesus dying 'for the sins of the world', we don't just mean that there was some kind of abstract theological transaction going on. We mean that the sins of the world, specific instances of some of the nastiest things that human beings can do to one another, happened to him directly. He wasn't immune to the normal human emotions. He didn't just ride it out without caring. He was the very embodiment of vulnerable love. He took the worst that can be done, took it from every angle, and gave back only more love. When we are betrayed, or treated unjustly or violently, we react angrily and often seek immediate vengeance. It is part of the inner core of meaning of Jesus' death that he didn't do that. He took the worst that evil could do. He allowed it to do its worst to him, emotionally as well as physically. And he went on loving.

Now I don't know how many of you have been betrayed, or have felt betrayed. I certainly don't know if any of you have ever betrayed someone else, someone you love or who loved and trusted you. But I do know, to keep this at a safe and general level for the moment, that the community of Easington has felt badly betrayed: betrayed by successive governments; betrayed by various politicians; betrayed, I dare say, by some of the leaders of the miners' movement itself. There are all kinds of bits and pieces of anger and resentment still around in communities like this, and betrayal is an accusation one hears quite frequently by people who have lost their livelihood, their way of life, their pension perhaps, certainly the prospects they once thought they had. What are we going to do about that?

Well, you can always cling on to it and live your life enjoying your status as a victim. Having someone else to blame means you can keep the high moral ground as long as you like. It's their fault; it's his fault; it's her fault; it's everyone's fault except (of course) mine. And this is a game we all play now and then, some more than others, not just about the state of our communities but about a thousand and one things great and small.

And part of the meaning of the cross is that Jesus died to take all that away. Underneath the story in John, once more, is the poem in Isaiah, this time the third of the Servant Songs. It has that very vivid description of the Servant giving his back to the people who were beating him, and his cheeks to those who were torturing him by pulling out his beard. He is totally vulnerable.

But in the next lines he is totally vindicated: God has been with him, and all those who were out to get him will find they are put in the wrong. Somehow he has taken the worst that evil people can do to him and has come through and out the other side. It's breathtaking but it's real. Somehow the Servant absorbs into himself all the evil that has taken place, trusting God that this is how it has to be, and God vindicates him.

What that means for us – and this is quite close to the heart of the meaning of the cross – is that the bad things that have happened in our lives, to us personally, or in our community, to our way of life, can be brought to the foot of the cross and left there. He has taken them: lies, injustices, betrayals, insults, physical violence, the lot. He meant to take them, because, in his great love for us, he did not intend that our lives should be crippled by them. Even when we have been partly responsible for them; in fact, particularly when we have been responsible for them. That's what forgiveness is all about: not saying 'It didn't really happen' or 'It didn't really matter' but rather 'It did happen, and it did matter, but Jesus has dealt with it all and we can be free of it.' Jesus didn't want us to be bowed down under that weight, turning us into grumblers and blamers and moaners. He wanted to take all that evil and set us free from its weight.

And now we see that part of the challenge of walking through Holy Week with John in one hand and Isaiah in the other is that we are called to forgive. We are called to forgive the people who've let us down, the systems that have let us down, the people and organizations and structures that have hurt us and people we love, that have done bad and callous and betraying things to us and our friends and have walked away laughing. Now, we add all of that together, all the wrong done here and all the frustration and sadness of recent decades, and we place it before the foot of the cross. Now, we name and shame the things that have defaced our community, and we weave them into the story of Jesus alongside Judas, alongside Caiaphas, alongside Pilate. And we pray that over the coming days we will have grace and strength to leave them there, to believe that Jesus has dealt with them on the cross. And we wait, as the disciples waited without knowing what they were waiting for, to see what God will do next once the cross has done its work.

There is more to the meaning of the cross than just this: much, much more. We will spend a lifetime exploring that further meaning. But for now, for the moment, let's gather up all the betrayal that has blighted our lives and see Jesus taking it on himself, in and through the action of Judas, so that we don't need to hold on to it any more. Let's pray for grace to forgive, to find new starts, to know that we have been vindicated by Jesus' vindication – and, beyond even that, that we are loved for ever within Jesus' great and powerful suffering love.

5

A SERMON AT THE EUCHARIST ON MAUNDY THURSDAY

Easington Colliery mass grave, 1951

The meal that says it all
(Exodus 12.1–14; 1 Corinthians 11.23–29; John 13.1–17, 31b–35)

———◆———

We have been thinking in the last four chapters, as we have walked together through the first part of Holy Week, of the way in which the story of Jesus functions like a great tune. We listen to it, and then we have to try to put in our bits of the harmony. (I suppose, having talked about harmonizing with the song all week, I shouldn't have been surprised that I got roped in to sing last night when some of the lads were having a folk evening over the other side of the street.)

Part of the way we know what the harmony ought to be is that we have the bass part, which we call the Old Testament. That keeps our feet on the ground, musically and theologically speaking. It stops us interpreting the story of Jesus any which way we like. And our job is to look out for the two middle parts: the tenor part, which is the story of our whole community, and the alto part, which is our bit, our own personal story somehow held in the middle of it all. And we've seen, in previous chapters, the way in which the story of Jesus, and its bass part in the book of Isaiah, invites us to bring the pains and anger of our community, and our own hearts, and allow them to be folded within the larger story, to be sung in tune with the passion of Jesus, so that we can learn to grieve, to go through the bereavement process for all that has been and all that has gone, and so to be ready for whatever new things God is going to do.

But it's at this point that the idea of this four-part song as a simple hymn-tune turns out to be a bit more complicated. To keep it as simple as I can, it's not just a hymn any more. This hymn, like some of the hymns for children, has actions that go with it. But, unlike the action songs that children sing, in this song it looks as though the actions are the real bit, the bit that matters, and the song is the accompaniment, instead of the other way around.

That's how it ought to be. Because when God came to us in Jesus, he didn't come to fill our heads with nice ideas, or even to fill our hearts with a new warmth and gratitude. He came to heal the world. He came to change the bad things that were happening and to make good things happen instead. He came to do that for individuals and also for communities. And when people are being sorted out, and when families and communities are getting themselves back in shape, one of the most central and important things they do is have a meal together. And that's exactly what Jesus did.

You see, when Jesus wanted to explain to his followers what his death was going to be all about – and they hadn't even really cottoned on to the fact that he was going to die yet, so he had to take it slowly – he didn't give them a theory, an explanation to hold simply in their heads. Oh, there was plenty for the heads to be working on, but that would take time. What he gave them instead was something to do: a meal to share, with a special bit that would tell his story more powerfully than any other way.

And of course that meal, that Last Supper, on the first Maundy Thursday, was, like everything with Jesus, a tune with an Old Testament bass part. We heard the bass part in our first reading: the story of the Passover, when God rescued the Israelites from slavery in Egypt and, as a sign, 'passed over' their houses on the night of judgment, because of the blood of the lamb on the doorposts. Jesus quite deliberately chose Passover as the moment to go up to Jerusalem and confront the authorities with the claims of God's kingdom, knowing what would happen.

He deliberately chose this Passover meal as the framework to give his followers, from that day to this, a way not simply of understanding his death, but of being healed, forgiven, renewed and transformed by it. Passover spoke powerfully of God rescuing his people, making them his own in a new way, and sending them off on the risky journey to their promised land. Jesus' new Passover speaks even more powerfully of God now rescuing his people in a full and final way, making them his own in a new and complete way, and sending them out into the world with the risky task of making his kingdom happen.

And this is the point at which the top line of music and the bass part – the story of Jesus and the Old Testament Passover tradition – insist on particular actions, not just ideas, for us to do. For a start, obviously, we go on day by day and week by week breaking bread and pouring out wine in remembrance of him. And it's important to remember what is happening when we do that. St Paul declares that 'every time you eat this bread and drink the cup, you proclaim the death of the Lord until he comes' (1 Corinthians 11.26).

And he doesn't just mean that the Breaking of Bread is a good moment for a sermon on the cross, though that may often be the case. He means that when you do this – even if it's just two or three of you here, or in an old people's home, or with a crowd in a cathedral, wherever – you are actually announcing to the world around, to the principalities and powers that keep people enslaved and fearful and angry, that Jesus is Lord, and that his death has broken the power of sin and fear and sorrow and shame. This meal is therefore simultaneously part of our journey through bereavement, acting out the dying of Jesus within which our own sorrows can be held and dealt with, and also part of our mission, because it is the powerful declaration that on the cross of Jesus Christ the living God has dealt with all that distorts and defaces human life. And this meal therefore propels us out, to go into the community in the confidence that God is at work, that Jesus is Lord, that the Spirit can and does heal and renew.

And that's why Maundy Thursday is such an important moment, both on the journey to the cross and already as the beginning of the life and mission of the church. The word 'Maundy' comes from a Latin word which means 'commandment', because at that Last Supper Jesus gave them a new commandment, to love one another as he had loved them.

Once more, he didn't just *tell* them to. He did it himself, and showed them how to do it. In some churches, on Maundy Thursday, they wash one another's feet to recapture something of that sense of love-in-action. That's the point: *it's all about the actions*, and the tune supports them rather than the other way around. Jesus went out from the Last Supper to give himself up, literally and physically, for his friends and for the whole world. He wants us to find out what we can and should be doing, actually doing, to make his kingdom known in the world.

Now we'll come back to this on Easter morning, because that's of course where the church's mission really gets going. But let's take this action-song just one step further. Here we are, with the Last Supper and Jesus' astonishing action of washing the disciples' feet, and saying 'Now you've seen it, go and do it.' And here is our ground bass part, the Passover story which is all about God setting people free from slavery. Now let's ask ourselves: Where is there slavery of some sort or other within a mile of where we are this evening, and what is God doing about it?

The answer isn't far away. There are people in the Colliery – I've met some of them – who have lost hope and are angry and bitter. There are young people who are in virtual slavery to drink, drugs and sex and the long-term prospect of getting trapped in unemployment. There are old people who are afraid to go out because of what's happening on the streets where they've lived all their lives. And we need to ask, in relation to all of them: What would it look like for them to be set free from that slavery? And how can our celebration of Jesus' strange new Passover equip us to be part of that answer?

And then, once more, for ourselves. We've been reading about bringing things to the foot of the cross – memories, sorrows, hopes and fears, anger, illness, puzzles. And we shall do that in one particular way, on Good Friday. But the Breaking of Bread is itself the classic, regular way of doing just that.

When I was a student chaplain I often had to listen to all kinds of stories of sorrow and anger as my young folk found their lives in a mess of one sort or another. I knew I didn't have the answers. But I also knew that if they would only come to the Lord's Table, bring their problems there, offer them up with open hands and then receive Jesus' own life in return, there was the strong hope of freedom, of change, of healing, of transformation. I pray that it may be so with us.

And remember: again and again, when God is up to something new, it doesn't always start with a bang. If God is going to hear our prayers in Holy Week and do new things in the Colliery, and in our lives, by our working through our sense of loss and bereavement in the light of the story of Jesus, it pretty certainly isn't going to mean that suddenly hundreds of people are going to flood into church, hundreds of new houses are going to be built, crime and drugs will stop and all the problems out there and in here are going to be solved at a stroke. No. Jesus often told parables about sowing seeds, about things growing secretly, little by little. There are signs of hope already. Some new things are happening in the community, and in the church. Other things may be starting up if you know where to look. Our job is to bring the whole thing, the 'out there' stuff and the 'in here' stuff, all of it, to the meal which speaks of the cross. And as we sow the seeds of prayer and faith; as we wait in the darkness of Maundy

Thursday; as we stand at the foot of the cross itself – we wait with hope, because the one whose journey we are sharing is the one who, as John says, loved his own who were in the world, and loved them to the end.

6

A SERMON
ON GOOD FRIDAY

THIS TABLET IS ERECTED TO THE MEMORY OF
EIGHTY THREE MEN WHO GAVE THEIR LIVES IN THE
EASINGTON COLLIERY DISASTER
TWENTY NINTH MAY NINETEEN HUNDRED & FIFTY ONE

SEVENTY TWO GRAVES ARE IN THIS CEMETERY
THE FOLLOWING NINE MEN ARE BURIED ELSEWHERE
FREDERICK CARR · RICHARD CHAMPLEY · JOSEPH GODSMAN
ERNEST GOYNS · HERBERT GOYNS · JOHN HARKER
JOHN WM HENDERSON · STANLEY PEACEFUL · STEPHEN WILSON

ALSO TO THE MEMORY OF TWO BRAVE MEN
JOHN YOUNG WALLACE AND HENRY BURDESS
WHO GAVE THEIR LIVES IN PERFORMANCE OF DUTIES
AS RESCUE WORKERS AND WHO ARE BURIED ELSEWHERE

Mass grave (memorial stone)

'It is finished'
(Isaiah 52.13—53.12;
John 19.16b–37)

———•◆•———

I don't know if any of you have ever been white-water canoeing. I confess it's been quite a long time since I did it, but there is one memory which stands out, a memory of a recurring theme which is really central to the whole experience. When you're in the canoe you are of course very low down on the water, and when you approach the rapids on a river you can't actually see over the edge of the waterfall. All you can see is flat water, and then nothing – though you can often hear the roar from the rushing water beyond. And somewhere on that edge where the water disappears you see a kind of inverted V-shape, with the water coming together at a particular point; and you know that that's the centre of the main stream, the point you have to aim for. If you hit the rapids anywhere else you'll probably be going down them sideways, which is not a very good idea. So you head for the place where the water is all rushing together, and the next thing you know you're in the middle of that frantic, turbulent white water.

Good Friday is a bit like that. We have been following Jesus along the way, through the comparatively smooth water, but now we hear the roar up ahead and we know: This Is It. And the only thing we can do is to watch for the way all the themes converge at this point, and go to the V-shape where they meet, not knowing what will happen to us as the cataclysmic events of Good Friday overtake us.

You see, although there are ways of making sense of Jesus' crucifixion, and we'll get to them in a moment, the first thing we should recognize is that for Jesus' followers and family at the time it made no sense at all. It was the denial of everything they'd longed for, the stupid and pointless snuffing out of the brightest light and best hope Israel had ever had. Jesus' crucifixion must have made his followers wonder if Satan had been tricking them all along, if God had not after all been at work in Jesus, if Israel's God was maybe not the world's creator and judge after all, if maybe Israel's God didn't exist, if maybe there was no God at all . . . Watching Jesus get dragged off to a mockery of a trial, a brutal and degrading beating and then the worst torture and death imaginable would force all those questions on them. If we don't recognize that, then we have domesticated the cross, turned it into a safe symbol of private faith, and forgotten what it was really all about. And then we wonder why we are left with nowhere to turn when things in our own lives, our own families, our own communities, our own civilization, seem to go not just pear-shaped – at least a pear still has a shape! – but utterly chaotic, totally random. Good Friday was chaos come again: darkness, earthquake, violence and the death of the one who had given life to so many.

If you've followed this book so far you'll see where this is going. Part of the task of those who heard the original talks was to walk the way of the cross in a kind of representative fashion on behalf of the entire community, a community that has seen chaos replace order and fear replace hope. That is where many people today live all the time.

It all seems so pointless, such a futile waste. Towns today invent 'neighbourhood watch' schemes; but you didn't need to invent one in Easington Colliery 15 years ago. The whole town was one neighbourhood. Everyone, in the best sense, was watching out for everyone else. Now, in a town where not so long ago people didn't lock their front doors, the same people are afraid to walk down the street, or to open their shops first thing in the morning in case there's someone lurking there waiting to burst in. And what I've been asking you to do all through is to look at this story of chaos and futility, and hold it in your imagination and prayers within the story of Jesus as he goes to the cross. And now, on Good Friday itself, we shall take the basketful of sorrows that we have prepared earlier and place them on the cross itself, as a sign of our wanting simply to put our chaos somehow alongside and inside God's chaos.

But of course as soon as we call it God's chaos we are making a statement of faith, a statement which has echoes of the Psalms and the prophets who looked at the ruin of Israel, at famine and disaster and devastation, and clung on with their fingernails to the belief that God was still God even if it really didn't look like that. Today we heard perhaps the best-known Old Testament passage of all: the fourth Servant Song, the end of Isaiah 52 and the whole of Isaiah 53.

It might be a good idea to read that song through slowly again, asking God to help you listen to the notes that it's playing and to think through the harmonies you need to fill in. It is a song about horrible violence, leaving the victim unrecognizable and scarcely human. It's a song about suffering so acute that people are ashamed and embarrassed and look away. It's a song about massive injustice, oppression doing its worst and getting away with it. Is it any wonder the first Christians saw it as a song about Jesus? But it's also, of course, a song about astonishing vindication, about suffering bearing fruit, about the sufferer seeing fruit from all the travail of his soul, and about a new work of God which springs up just when all seemed lost in darkness and futility.

And it is all this because it is a song about the substitute. It's about the king who stands in for his people and does for them what they can't do for themselves. It's about the prophet seeing and speaking God's purpose and word for the people that couldn't see or speak it themselves. It's about the priest who enters the holy place alone on behalf of the people. Is it any wonder the first Christians saw it as a song about Jesus? And at its heart there is the terrifying theme which we approach with caution, because like white-water rapids it can turn us upside down and crash us against the rocks, and yet which we can't avoid because it stands at the heart of Jesus' own understanding of his vocation. 'He was wounded for our transgressions; he was bruised for our iniquities; upon him was the punishment which made us whole, and by his bruises we are healed. All we like sheep have gone astray; we have all turned to our own way; and the Lord has laid on him the iniquity of us all' (Isaiah 53.5–6).

And that is why, of course, before we even get to the tune, to John's gospel itself once more, we have to pause and whisper the alto part which is our own bit of the harmony. Faced with that bass line, the only thing we can say is, Thank you; thank you; nothing in my hand I bring, simply to thy cross I cling; when I survey the wondrous cross, where the young prince of glory died, my richest gain I count but loss, and pour contempt on all my pride. Thankfully we have poets who have said it better than we can. We share their words, and hope to grow more into them. But the only proper response to the death of Jesus, wounded for our transgressions and bruised for our iniquities, is gratitude, faith and love.

And, as we look up in that gratitude, we allow ourselves to see Jesus hanging there on the first Good Friday. We see him once more with John's eyes.

First, John says, he is the king. Pilate put up the sign saying so, and refused to alter it. But the king is the one who stands in for his people, like David fighting Goliath on behalf of Israel. Jesus is off to meet the giant, the forces of chaos and death, on our behalf.

Jesus is, second, the one in whom the suffering Psalms find their fulfilment. People gamble for his clothing, and mock his thirst with sour wine.

And he is the true Passover Lamb. His bones are not to be broken.

John is telling us all this. It would, again, be a good thing to read the whole of John 19 slowly once more. But in the middle of it, at verse 30, there stands one word which says it all. 'Finished.' 'Accomplished.' 'Completed.' Jesus' last word, which sums it all up. Part of its meaning is that everything that had gone before – all the lines of water that came rushing towards that great V-shape – has now come together. This is where it was all going; this is what it was all about.

Part of its meaning is that in Jesus' world that word 'finished' was what you wrote on a bill when it had been settled: 'Paid in full!' But underneath these is the meaning John intends, I believe, most deeply. When God the creator made his wonderful world, at the end of the sixth day he finished it. He completed his work. Now, on the Friday, the sixth day of the week, Jesus has completed the work of redeeming the world. With his shameful, chaotic, horrible death he has gone to the very bottom, to the darkest and deepest place of ruin, and has planted there the sign that says 'Rescued'. It is the sign of love, the love of the creator for his ruined creation, the love of the saviour for his ruined people. Yes, of course, it all has to be worked out. The victory has to be implemented. But it's done; it's completed; it's finished.

And where do we come in? Perhaps we can see ourselves in the figures of Mary and John, standing at the foot of the cross. Mary's life was never going to be the same again: the son she adored, the one on whom she had rested all her hope and delight, was killed. John's life was never going to be the same again: the Master he adored, who had made him his special companion, was gone. But through the cross Jesus provided a new identity, a new community in miniature, for both of them, in one another. Now here in this community, and in this church, there are plenty of Marys and Johns, plenty of people for whom life isn't going to be the same again. Our job is to stand and wait at the foot of the cross, and to see what fresh word may come to us concerning the way forward, the way of becoming a community again.

I don't know what that will mean in practice. But I do know that if we can't find the answer in the cross, we won't find it anywhere else. Good Friday is the point at which God comes into our chaos, to be there with us in the middle of it and to bring us his new creation. Let us pause and give thanks, and listen for his words of love and healing.

7

A MEDITATION
ON HOLY SATURDAY

Memorial Avenue

Waiting
(Lamentations 1.1–22;
John 19.28–42)

———•◆•———

I was struck in a new way, while preparing these talks, by the book we call the Lamentations of Jeremiah. Lamentations is what you'd get if you walked up and down the streets of your city or town and allowed yourself to be totally open to, totally aware of, the violence and squalor and sadness all around. And the church from quite early on has seen the Lamentations of Jeremiah as a kind of long-range advance prophetic poem about the sheer desolation and sorrow of Good Friday and Holy Saturday. 'Is it nothing to you, all you who pass by? Look and see if there is any sorrow like my sorrow . . .' (Lamentations 1.12a). It is the sheer awful pointlessness, the hopelessness of it all, that should overwhelm us at this time, like the prophet looking around Jerusalem, which had been full of people going about normal life, a thriving town in all directions, and seeing instead devastation, ruin, families torn apart, utter hopelessness.

Jeremiah expresses all this with an unmatched sense of sorrow and despair. But, as he does so, he does two other things as well with this sorrow which stand out quite strikingly. First, and most noticeable, he insists that God is in this too. *You* have done this, he says. *You* have brought us to this point. *You* have allowed all this to come upon us. Now you might think that this was a pretty dark view of God, and in a sense it is. But the point is that only by clinging on to the sovereignty of God is there still hope. If you say that God has no idea what's going on either, and is just as helpless as we feel, then things are bleak indeed.

But of course to say that God is in all this somewhere, when everything seems hopeless, is to say quite simply that we don't know what God is up to. It is to commit ourselves to waiting; waiting without any sense of being able to see how it's all going to turn out, or even if it is at all. It is to learn, at quite a deep level, the lesson our generation is peculiarly bad at learning, the lesson of patience. And out of this relentless insistence on God's presence in the middle of the darkness Jeremiah does indeed get to hope in the end; but it's a hard-won hope, a new-born hope, a different sort of hope from what he would have had before.

The second thing Jeremiah does, less noticeable for us but still very powerful, is the way he writes the book. You know how as children you learn things by the alphabet – A is for Apple, B is for Bear, C is for Cat, and so on? Well, like some other Hebrew poets Jeremiah wrote out his lamentations, his weeping and wailing for the chaos that had come over Jerusalem, with each verse of the poem beginning with the next letter of the alphabet. He goes through the alphabet four times in the first four chapters of the book, and then Chapter 5 is a prayer which rounds things off. Do you see the point? Do you see what he's doing?

He isn't just playing word games, showing how clever he is. The alphabet is the very ancient way of saying that the various sounds we make when we speak are not random and chaotic. There is a pattern, a form, underneath it all. So at the very moment when Jeremiah is saying in his poem, 'This doesn't make sense! There's no meaning to all this! Why should this be happening?' he is expressing that outburst of desperate grief in a form which says, 'And yet I believe it isn't random; I believe there is meaning and purpose, even though I can't see it at all just now.' He can see nothing but chaos and ruin all around, but he has expressed that in a pattern which says, 'And yet I trust that somewhere, somehow, there is order after all.' The challenge of the Old Testament, again and again, is to go on believing in God's order even when everything seems utterly meaningless, with hope gone and chaos come again.

Lamentations is of course one segment of what, this week, I've been calling the bass part, the bottom line of music, for understanding the tune of Jesus' path to the cross and now the awful sense of desolation after Jesus has died and been buried. The book of Job merely confirms that sense of desolation: cut down a tree, and it may sprout up again, but once a man dies, that's it (Job 14.7–12). And though some other Old Testament writers inch towards a belief in resurrection, Job is right – in terms of the present creation and the way it works. If there is anything else to come, any real hope, it will need a whole new creation.

And with Good Friday there is still no sign of such a thing. And all we can do on Holy Saturday is therefore to say, with Lamentations, 'Yes, this is awful; this is beyond belief; it is chaos come again; but we will sit quietly and wait. All we can believe is that, though we can see nothing, no signs of hope, God is still the God of order and not chaos, and he will do what he will do.' This day, the quiet, sad day between Good Friday and Easter, finds us in the position of the two disciples on the road to Emmaus, who said, 'We had hoped that he was the one to redeem Israel' – with the sense of, 'But he can't have been, because they killed him.' That sense of puzzlement – a puzzlement which we all know only too well in many aspects of our personal lives, and of our community, with all its echoes of Jeremiah's Lamentations – is the classic Holy Saturday place to be. We have expressed our sorrow and anger, and we have brought it to the cross and will leave it there. Now we must wait quietly to see what God will do.

Arguably the greatest poem by arguably the greatest twentieth-century English poet contains a passage which speaks powerfully about this waiting.

> I said to my soul, be still, and wait without hope
> For hope would be hope for the wrong thing; wait without
>   love
> For love would be love of the wrong thing; there is yet faith
> But the faith and the love and the hope are all in the waiting.
> Wait without thought, for you are not ready for thought:
> So the darkness shall be the light, and the stillness the
>   dancing . . .
>
>   In order to arrive there,
> To arrive where you are, to get from where you are not,
>   You must go by a way wherein there is no ecstasy.
> In order to arrive at what you do not know
>   You must go by a way which is the way of ignorance.
> In order to possess what you do not possess
>   You must go by the way of dispossession.
> In order to arrive at what you are not
>   You must go through the way in which you are not.

That's T. S. Eliot, in the second of his *Four Quartets*. And I suggest that it is a true Holy Saturday perception. Jesus' disciples knew what they had been hoping for, and it was all gone. They had hoped for a thoroughly earthly kingdom, with Jesus as king and themselves in the top jobs. Forget it: wait without hope, for hope would be hope for the wrong thing. All their ambitions for their people, their land, their towns, their homes: forget it. Wait without love, for love would be love of the wrong thing. Some of them, on that first Holy Saturday, must have been thinking frantically: How can we make sense of it all? What on earth has gone so badly wrong? Why should this have happened? Forget it: wait without thought, for you are not ready for thought. Holy Saturday is the moment when everything stops and waits.

And waits – for a different kind of answer. If you want God's hope instead of yours; if you want God's love instead of yours; if you want God's thoughts instead of yours – then you will need to go through a time of silence, of resting, of ignorance and dispossession. And if we want to find God's way forward for this community, for ourselves, for this church – and we are, in many respects, a microcosm of where so many churches up and down our country are today – then we must learn to wait, to be quiet, to affirm God's order in our chaos but not yet to understand it. Only when, in days and years and decades to come, people look back and see the new things that God will have done, things we can't at the moment imagine or plan for, we will say, 'Yes: we needed to let go of that anger and grief, to leave it on the cross of Jesus, to see it buried in his tomb; because God's new creation is God's new creation, always a surprise, always a shock.'

Holy Saturday is therefore the sabbath rest after the completion of the work of redemption. Remember how, at the end of the creation account in Genesis, we are told that when God finished all his work on the sixth day he rested on the seventh day. Now John has brought Jesus' redeeming work to its completion, with that great word 'It is finished' as Jesus dies. Hold in your mind all that it means for the Jesus of John's gospel to die: the Word of God, falling silent; the living water, no longer flowing; the bread from heaven, scattered in the long grass; the light of the world, snuffed out; the good shepherd, snatched away from the flock; the grain of wheat, falling into the earth and dying; the Messiah coming to his own people and his own rejecting him. Put them all together, and see them folded in this deep and dark sabbath rest, this seventh day, waiting as we must wait for whatever God will do and bring:

> On the seventh day God rested in the darkness of the tomb,
> Having finished on the sixth day all his work of joy and doom;

A meditation on Holy Saturday

Now the Word had fallen silent, and the water had run dry,
The bread had all been broken, and the light had left the sky;
The flock had lost its shepherd, and the seed was sadly sown,
The courtiers had betrayed their king, and nailed him to his
   throne.
O sabbath rest by Calvary, O calm of tomb below,
Where the grave-clothes and the spices cradle him we did not
   know!
Rest you well, beloved Jesus: Caesar's Lord and Israel's King,
In the brooding of the Spirit, in the darkness of the spring.

8

A SERMON FOR
THE EASTER MORNING
EUCHARIST

Seaside Lane

New heavens, new earth
(Isaiah 65.17–25; Acts 10.34–43;
John 20.1–18)

Today is not the end. It is the beginning.

Yes, I grant you this is the end of the bit of the journey you and I have been making together. It is always a wonderful thing to share a pilgrimage through Holy Week, and to think and pray with friends as we follow Jesus to the cross and the tomb. And often Easter does feel like the end of the story, of that particular journey.

Well, it isn't. It's just the beginning. Actually, I do think we in the church sell ourselves short on this one. We've kept the Forty Days of Lent; we've walked the Holy Week path; we've been attentive to Jesus' story for the last three days in particular. And now what we really should do is to have a forty-day party, or maybe even a fifty-day one, all the way through to Pentecost. If we've given something up for Lent, or even if we haven't, we should certainly take something up for Easter. But how you do that is up to you. My job now is to help you celebrate the first day of God's new creation.

Because, you see, that's what it's all about. The gospels don't really reach a conclusion. They point on to something more that's still to come. But what is this 'something more'? What is Easter all about? And how can it help us find the hope we need that's going to give us energy for the fresh tasks that lie ahead of us now, here in this community?

This is where many Christians have gone wrong, mainly because they haven't been listening to the music. We've been talking about the tune which is the story of Jesus, the bass part which is the Old Testament background, and the middle parts which are about us and our world. Well, too many Christians have listened to the tune about Jesus' resurrection and they have assumed that it's supposed to harmonize with a bass part that says that the point of it all is simply to go to heaven when you die. Jesus died and went to heaven, and so will we. But that's not what the Easter stories are about at all. It's hard to get our heads around this, so let's take it step by step.

Many of you will have driven up to Northumberland through the Tyne Tunnel. Now supposing a child saw you stopped in a traffic queue in Jarrow, and asked where you were going, and you said 'Northumberland'. She would then see you driving off into the tunnel, and she might think that Northumberland was inside the tunnel. But she'd be wrong. First you go down into the tunnel, and then, later, you come up the other side, into the sunlight and into the new county. (Actually, I know they've now invented a new county, 'Tyne and Wear', which straddles the river, but those of us who grew up in the north-east some years ago still think in terms of Northumberland on the north of the Tyne and County Durham on the south.)

It's the same with what happens after death. People sometimes talk as if 'resurrection' was what happened at once, as soon as you die. It isn't. Jesus died on Good Friday and he wasn't raised from the dead until three days later. Where was he in between? Well, in Luke's gospel he says to the thief, 'Today you'll be with me in Paradise.' 'Paradise' isn't the final destination. It's the time of rest and bliss which God's people pass through in order to get to the final destination. This is where the illustration of the tunnel isn't quite so helpful, because the tunnel is dark and gloomy, whereas the Paradise we are promised is a place of light and rest for God's people. But the point is that Paradise isn't your final destination. So all talk of simply 'going to heaven', as though that were the end of the story, isn't going to help.

Where *are* we heading, then? Go back to the bass part, to the Old Testament: and, once more, we're in Isaiah. Isaiah speaks of *new heavens and new earth* – and the New Testament writers pick this up in various ways. The way it seems to work is like this. When God made this lovely world, he wasn't making junk. He doesn't want to throw it away and do something completely different, as though the idea of space, time and matter was a bad one from the start. No: he wants to abolish, from within this world, everything that corrupts and defaces and distorts his beautiful creation, so that he can give the world a giant makeover. New heavens and new earth – like the present one only with everything that's true and beautiful and lovely made even better, and everything that's bad and sad and degrading abolished for ever. That's what we're promised. Read Isaiah 65 again and see.

And that's why 'resurrection' is what matters, rather than just 'going to heaven'. Oh, if you belong to Jesus you will go to heaven to be with him; that's what 'Paradise' means. But that's just the long, bright tunnel before the new county begins. And when God makes new heavens and new earth, he will raise you from the dead and give you a new body so that you can live in that new world – and, indeed, help God to run it. That's the deal; that's what the New Testament promises, even though many generations of Christians have never even begun to realize it.

Now we come to the point. When Jesus was raised from the dead on the first Easter day, it wasn't simply as though he'd gone on ahead of us through the tunnel and out the other side. It is, rather, as though the Duke of Northumberland were suddenly to appear in the middle of County Durham, plant his flag here, and say, 'This bit already belongs to me; there's a bit of Northumberland right here.' In other words, in Jesus' resurrection *a bit of God's future, of God's new heaven and earth, has come forward in time.* You've seen the film *Back to the Future*?

Well, the point of the resurrection is that at Easter a bit of the future – God's promised future – has come forwards to meet us, 'back to the present'.

I know many people find this confusing, so let me try and say it a different way and see if it helps. You know that when it's ten o'clock in the evening here it's already ten o'clock in the morning in Australia? Perhaps you have friends or relatives in Australia or New Zealand; sometimes they may phone you, forgetting what time it is here, and they wake you up in the middle of the night. Well, what happens with the resurrection is like this. This whole world is still in the old time – ten o'clock at night, if you like. Evil and death are still at work. We're all still asleep and we think nothing is ever going to be different. But suddenly we get, not a phone call, but a visit, from someone who is living in New Time. He is already in the new day. He has gone through death and out into God's new world, God's new creation, and to our astonishment he's come forwards into our world, which is still in Old Time, to tell us that the day has in fact dawned and that even though we feel sleepy and it still seems dark out there the new world has begun and we'd better wake up and get busy.

And now at last, with this as clear as I can make it, we're ready to understand what was going on on that first Easter morning. Once you get the bass part straight, you may be able to understand the tune itself. 'Very early in the morning, while it was still dark, Mary Magdalene came to the tomb . . .' (John 20.1); and she ran, and Peter and John ran, and they were flustered and worried and puzzled and scared, because this was something they were totally unready for, something they'd never imagined.

For them, the idea of 'resurrection' had, up to that point, been quite simple. It was, they would have said, what would happen to everyone at the end – when everyone got through the tunnel to the other side, if you like, or when the day finally dawned and the Old Time was abolished for ever. Only gradually, and particularly when they met Jesus, with his body fully alive, indeed, more alive than it had ever been, because it had been through death and out the other side – only gradually did they realize what had happened. *In his death, Jesus had taken all the sin and death and shame and sorrow of the world upon himself*, so that by letting it do its worst to him he had destroyed its power, which means that now there is nothing to stop the new creation coming into being. *Jesus' resurrection body is the first bit of the new creation, the sign of the new world that is to come.* In terms of Good Friday as the sixth day, and Holy Saturday as the seventh day, the day when God rested after creation, the day when Jesus rested after redemption, Easter Day is the eighth day, the first day of the new week. This isn't the end; it's the beginning.

And that is why Easter is the start of the church's mission. Let's be quite clear. The church's mission isn't about telling more and more people that if they accept Jesus they will go to heaven. That is true, as far as it goes (though we ought to be telling them about the new heavens and new earth rather than just 'heaven'), but it's not the point of our mission. The point is that if God's new creation has already begun, those of us who have been wakened up in the middle of the night are put to work *to make more bits of new creation happen within the world as it still is.* And that is why we need to leave behind, on the cross, all the bits and pieces of the old creation that have made us sad, that have depressed us and our communities, and start to pray for vision and wisdom to know where God can and will make new creation happen in our lives, in our hearts, in our homes and not least in our communities. That's what 'regeneration' is all about. This is where the middle parts of the music come into their own, our part and the community's part, between the great Easter tune on top and the promise of new creation down below.

Yes, I know, people will tell you it can't happen, that it's just a pious dream. That's what they said to all the great Christian workers from the earliest Christians through to William Wilberforce 200 years ago and Desmond Tutu 20 years ago. But the answer isn't better politics (though we need that too), nor better government funding (though that wouldn't go amiss), nor simply better youth work (and, yes, we need that too). The answer is that where God's people celebrate Jesus' resurrection they discover that new possibilities open up in front of them. That's why we renew and reaffirm our baptismal vows at Easter, to claim once more that we stand on resurrection ground, not just for ourselves but because of what God wants to do through us. We claim the victory of Jesus Christ over all that is evil, so that we can leave it behind on the cross and go forward to do new things in the power of his Spirit.

Now, I don't know what those new things might be. We can and do plan and pray and work for such things as we can see are needed immediately. But I would love to think that Christian people here in the Colliery would be part of the push to get something done about the old school, and perhaps replace it partly with a new recreation centre for everyone and partly with some new and affordable housing. I'd love to think of folk with their spiritual roots here in the church getting stuck in to the debates about how to create once more the kind of society where people trust each other and live together without fear. It's going to have to be rooted in prayer and in celebration of the lordship of Jesus; that's the only way to do it properly.

And it doesn't have to wait until you have more people coming to church, or more young families, though that would be nice. After all, Jesus began his work of new creation with one or two very puzzled women and a few frightened fishermen. In fact, one of the things about the way new creation works is that very often God seems to take special pleasure in doing things despite the fact that the human resources seem slim, not to say grossly inadequate. What matters is, as Bishop Jack Nicholls of Sheffield said at a conference two years ago, more prayer and more parties. More knocking on God's door to see what he wants us to be doing; and more celebrations of God's new creation, both here in church and wherever else you can.

I haven't answered all the questions. I haven't offered a blueprint for how to make this church, or any particular church, 'grow', or how to transform the Colliery, or any community, into a healthy, faithful, wise and humane town once again. (There are resources for that, not least the recent Church of England Report called *Faithful Cities*.) I haven't even given any suggestions for what to 'take up' this Easter season. That'll be for others to do, and for you to work out in prayer and under the guidance of the Spirit.

But what I hope I've done, at least in part, is to come with you on a journey through bereavement and grief to the foot of the cross, and to have planted some seeds of hope. And, as you remember from earlier chapters, the point about planting seeds is that you have no idea what they will do when they come up. What we do know is that Jesus Christ is risen from the dead, that God's new creation has begun, and that we have to do two things: first, to be true to our own baptismal vows to die with him and to share his new life, and, second, to allow his Spirit to work through us to make new creation happen in his world.